A HiSTORY OF AMERICaN crazes

FAD MANIA!

CYNTHIa OVERBECK BIX

TWENTY-FIRST CENTURY BOOKS / MINNEAPOLIS

To my wonderful husband, John, and son, Max, who provided
me with great ideas for fads from different generations and
listened patiently to my endless plans for this book

Twenty-First Century Books
A division of Lerner Publishing Group, Inc.
241 First Avenue North
Minneapolis, MN 55401 USA

For reading levels and more information, look up this title at www.lernerbooks.com.

Main text set in Conduit ITC Std 11/15. Typeface provided by International
Typeface Corp.

Library of Congress Cataloging-in-Publication Data

Bix, Cynthia Overbeck.
        Fad Mania! a history of American crazes / by Cynthia Overbeck Bix.
        pages   cm
        Includes bibliographical references and index.
        ISBN 978-1-4677-1034-3 (lib. bdg. : alk. paper)
        ISBN 978-1-4677-4793-6 (eBook)
        1. United States—Civilization—20th century—Juvenile literature. 2. United
States—Civilization—21st century—Juvenile literature. 3. Popular culture—
United States—History—20th century—Juvenile literature. 4. Popular culture—
United States—History—21st century—Juvenile literature. I. Title.
        E169.1.B56 2015
        973.91—dc23   2013034669

Manufactured in the United States of America
1 – PC – 7/15/14

CONTENTS

Fads are born to die.

—Ken Hakuta, *How to Create Your Own Fad and Make a Million Dollars, 1988*

CHAPTER ONE
Here Today, Gone Tomorrow

Have you ever heard of swallowing live goldfish? Streaking naked through a classroom? What about Cabbage Patch Kids? Or did you ever collect Webkinz or Silly Bandz?

Fads like these are wildly popular. They catch on suddenly and eventually die out. But while they are hot, they provide a snapshot of American popular culture. The rebellious spirit of 1920s youth, for example, expressed itself in a craze for dance marathons and the high-energy Charleston. Fads of the 1950s, including stuffing phone booths with as many people as possible, reflected that prosperous decade's readiness to relax and have fun. By the 1980s, new technology had brought the Pac-Man video-gaming craze from Japan to North America. Three decades later, another technology—the Internet—helped foster the flash mob craze. Through quick online organization, large numbers of people—a mob—could easily plan an event, get together in a public place, do something fun or crazy, and then move on.

Facing page: Americans have always loved a wild stunt. Swallowing live goldfish, a stunt launched by college students in the 1930s, was one of many crazes that have gripped the nation over the decades.

> "a fad is a form of energy, like thunder and lightning . . . . It takes on a life of its own, coursing through the veins of the country like a wonder drug."
>
> *—Richard A. Johnson,* **American Fads,** *1985*

FLASH IN THE PAN OR HERE TO STAY?

What starts out as a fad often turns into a long-lasting trend. Skateboarding is a good example. First introduced in the 1960s, skateboards were a craze, especially in California. Early wood or plastic skateboards were hard to maneuver, though, because they were mounted on hard clay wheels that tracked poorly. Sure enough, the fad died out. But in the 1970s, urethane wheels and lightweight, strong fiberglass bodies made skateboards super flexible. Helmets and kneepads and elbow pads provided protection, and soon, kids everywhere were doing eye-popping stunts. After that, skateboarding never really went away. Most cities have skate parks, and skateboarding has become a competitive sport on a professional level.

▲ Skateboarding started out as a fad in the 1960s and has hung on as a popular recreational activity ever since. This group takes to the streets of Chicago, Illinois, with their boards in 1965.

THE NEXT GREAT STYLE

In a special fad category are clothing fashions, which come and go but do so in a regular, systematic way. Every season brings new styles from fashion designers—short skirts or tight-fitting men's jackets or the color orange. We expect these styles to be very popular for a while, then to fade. But we also expect that new styles the next season will replace them. Many styles, such as T-shirts, become classics, but small modifications are always making them a little different. Similar cyclical fads include car designs, books, and movies. Today's blockbuster will always be replaced by the "next big thing."

MONEY + LEISURE = FADS GALORE

Fads in the United States are a modern phenomenon that became possible with increased leisure time. Around 1900 the average workweek was seventy hours, and many children labored up to twelve hours a day in factories. Then, with new labor laws allowing for time off, the weekend was born and people had time to have fun. In addition, the American middle class was growing as manufacturing expanded. Ordinary people were earning more money and could afford to buy the latest luxury. Everything from stylish clothing to toys to phonograph records was cheap and abundant. Advertising created demand for these goods. Ads on billboards and in daily newspapers encouraged people to buy bicycles and electric trains, baseball gloves and glittery jewelry. All these factors set the stage for a never-ending parade of fads and crazes.

Twenty-three skiddoo!

—H.A. Smith, a popular 1920s slang phrase meaning "Let's get out of here!"

CHAPTER TWO
DANCE TILL YOU DROP: THE ROARING TWENTIES

With the end of World War I in 1918, Americans were ready to have fun. The economy was booming, and more people could buy new clothes, home furnishings, and other goods at cheaper prices than ever before. Model T automobiles rolled off assembly lines, and housewives put aside their brooms for a new electric device called the vacuum cleaner.

Radio and movies provided entertainment on a mass scale for the first time in American history. Crazes in music, dance, and fashion swept the country. Goofy stunts and competitions seemed to be everywhere. If there was a record for the longest, the fastest, or the highest, Americans loved to watch somebody break it.

Facing page: Popular singer, dancer, and comedian Florence Mills (born Florence Winfrey) kicks up her heels in the Charleston in 1925. This dance craze started in the 1920s and paved the way for many dance crazes in future decades.

Milestones

World War I ends.

The Prohibition era begins when the US Congress ratifies the Eighteenth Amendment to the Constitution, prohibiting the sale, manufacture, and consumption of alcoholic beverages.

Congress ratifies the Nineteenth Amendment, giving American women the right to vote.

The first motion picture with sound is shown in New York City. Titled *Don Juan*, it stars the great stage actor John Barrymore in a swashbuckling role. Talkies quickly became all the rage.

The rapid expansion of radio includes the founding of NBC (National Broadcasting Company).

United Independent Broadcasters, later renamed CBS (Columbia Broadcasting System) is formed.

American pilot Charles Lindbergh makes the first-ever nonstop solo flight from New York to Paris, France. He becomes a national hero.

The Great Crash signals the beginning of the Great Depression, a global financial catastrophe that leaves millions of people out of work and world economies at an all-time low.

"AIN'T WE GOT FUN?"

A perky song called "Ain't We Got Fun?" summed up the attitude of the Roaring Twenties—an era alive with new, exciting music. Jazz musicians introduced the world to swinging rhythms and sounds, and along with the music came dance fads. Flappers in daring new dresses that barely covered their knees kicked up their heels. To do one dance—the shimmy—a dancer shimmied (or shook) her shoulders and her upper body in a move considered very risqué for women at the time. But the ultimate dance fad was the Charleston. To a lively beat, dancers sashayed sideways, hands moving from knee to knee, as they moved their feet—toes in, toes out— across the dance floor, adding stylish kicks for flair. For older dancers, used to waltzing gently, the Charleston was shockingly wild and fast-paced.

THE It GiRL

The wild young women of the 1920s, with their short hair, short skirts, and bright red lipstick, were nicknamed flappers. Movie star and sex symbol Clara Bow was the model for them all. Her role as an upbeat shop girl in the 1927 movie *It* earned her stardom and the nickname It Girl. Director Frank Lloyd said of her, "Bow is the personification of the ideal aristocratic flapper, mischievous, pretty, aggressive, quick-tempered and deeply sentimental."

This movie poster for the 1927 silent film *Hula*—a romantic comedy set in Hawaii—features the film's star, popular actress Clara Bow.

HOW LONG CAN THEY LAST?

Endurance contests took hold in the 1920s and into the 1930s. Legend has it that Alma Cummings started the dance marathon fad. She danced nonstop for 27 hours, outlasting six different partners. After that, local dance studios all over the country began holding dance marathon contests. Soon professional promoters staged contests, awarding prize money—usually a few hundred dollars—to the couple who could dance the longest. Not unlike audiences of TV reality shows, spectators rooted for their favorite couples and took perverse pleasure in watching their ordeal. A contest could go on for weeks. One event in Spokane, Washington, lasted 1,638 hours (more than two months), and others lasted even longer.

"HERE IN THE HALF-LIGHT THEY LIE, THESE SPRAWLING, UNCONSCIOUS FORMS, THEIR COTS SIDE BY SIDE, THEIR CLOTHING HUNG IN LISTLESS DISARRAY ... A GIRL IS SPRAWLED, HER LIPS MOVING IN PAIN .... BENDING OVER HER IS A MAN, HER 'TRAINER' ..., WHO MASSAGES HER SWOLLEN FEET WITH SOME OINTMENT."

—*"Dance Marathons of the 1920s and 1930s," 1928 newspaper article*

Dancers were allowed a short break every hour to lie down but otherwise had to keep moving. Men shaved using a mirror hung around their partners' neck. Often one partner supported the other while he or she took a nap. Promoters fed the dancers on chest-high tables so the contestants could eat while dancing. Many contestants went a little crazy from lack of sleep and privacy. They argued and even began to hallucinate, becoming hysterical while spectators watched.

Why did people put themselves through the humiliation and the strain? Some did it for laughs or on a dare. Some thought winning a contest might be a stepping-stone to fame and fortune. But with the economic collapse of the Great Depression (1929–1942), many entered the competitions for the food and the money. Dance marathons are still popular in the twenty-first century, although they usually last only forty-eight hours at most. And the money dancers earn usually goes to charitable causes.

HIGH CHAIR

You have heard of tree sitters, but flagpole sitters? In 1924 a movie promoter hired ex-sailor and stuntman Alvin "Shipwreck" Kelly to sit on top of a pole outside a Hollywood, California, movie theater. The thirteen-hour publicity stunt drew large crowds, who then bought movie tickets. Once newspapers got hold of the story, a nationwide craze was born. From teenage boys to grown men seeking publicity, daring participants tried to set records. Fifteen-year-old Avon Foreman of Baltimore, Maryland, did not have a flagpole handy. So he climbed an 18-foot (5.5-meter) tree in his backyard for his flagpole sit of ten days, ten hours, ten minutes, and ten seconds. "Phantom of the Flagpole"

Alvin "Shipwreck" Kelly on a 39-foot (12 m) flagpole in Newark, New Jersey. Beating his previous seven-day record, he sat on a 20-inch-wide (51 centimeters) seat with coffee, water, and reading material for twelve days in the summer of 1927.

Robert Hull sat on a pole for eighteen days. Some girls and women got into the act, too. Bobbie Mack, a twenty-one-year-old stunt airplane flier, sat atop a pole in Los Angeles, California, for twenty-one days.

Flagpole sitters often used boards for balance or even set up a chair atop the pole. Shipwreck Kelly had a wooden seat covered in leather. Atop his pole, he shaved, drank milk, coffee, and soup hoisted up to him in a bucket, and even read books. (It is not recorded how he managed to go to the bathroom!) During his flagpole-sitting career, Kelly logged a total of 20,613 hours aloft.

By the end of the 1920s, the flagpole-sitting craze was over. Kelly died penniless. His body was found on the streets of New York City. His pockets were empty—except for a bundle of tattered newspaper clippings about his once-famous stunts.

"WONDER TOY"

These disks on a string have actually been around for centuries. But it took an enterprising young US immigrant from the Philippines (where yo-yos were already popular) to make them a smash hit in the United States. In Los Angeles, Pedro Flores began making handmade yo-yos out of wood, which he sold to local kids. In 1928 Flores founded the Yo-Yo Manufacturing Company and opened a factory to mass-produce the toys. Within the first year, the company was turning out three hundred thousand yo-yos a day.

Flores drummed up more interest in his product by staging yo-yo contests. Contestants did tricks such as "sleeping," "rock the baby," "around the world," and "walking the dog." Kids flocked to buy Flores's inexpensive Wonder Toy. Entrepreneur Donald F. Duncan Sr. saw a golden business opportunity and bought the yo-yo company from Flores around 1929. As the years went by, Duncan came out with yo-yos that whistled and that lit up. Plastic yo-yos joined the traditional wooden ones. *Yo-yo* became a household word—and they are still popular.

Twenty-first-century yo-yo contests feature sophisticated tricks and effects. In 2012 Wong Wai Sheuk Simpson of Hong Kong broke a world record at the World Yo-Yo Contest in Orlando, Florida. He threw a sleeper that lasted thirty minutes!

Nine-year-old pogo stick champ Donald Saboe Jr. of Baltimore, Maryland, bounces high in the air in the mid-1950s. The craze launched in the 1920s and had comebacks in later decades. ▶

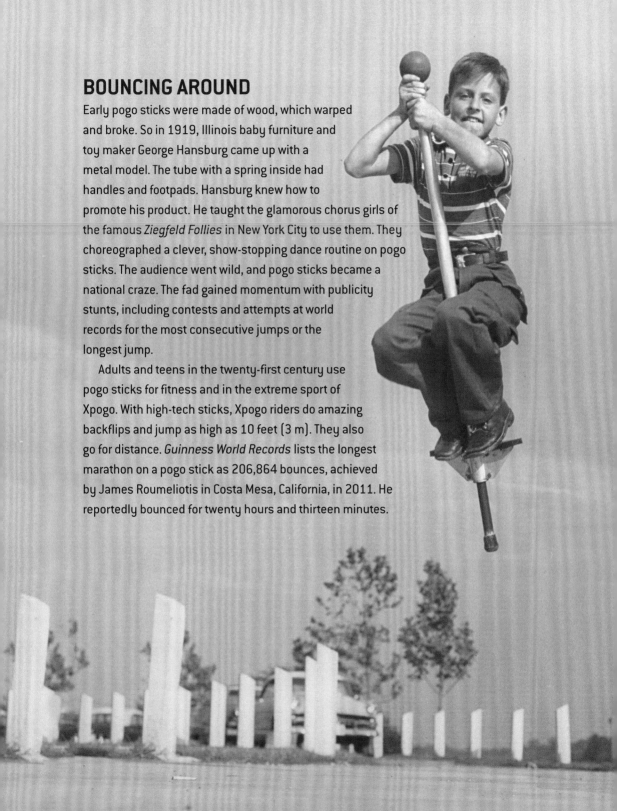

BOUNCING AROUND

Early pogo sticks were made of wood, which warped and broke. So in 1919, Illinois baby furniture and toy maker George Hansburg came up with a metal model. The tube with a spring inside had handles and footpads. Hansburg knew how to promote his product. He taught the glamorous chorus girls of the famous *Ziegfeld Follies* in New York City to use them. They choreographed a clever, show-stopping dance routine on pogo sticks. The audience went wild, and pogo sticks became a national craze. The fad gained momentum with publicity stunts, including contests and attempts at world records for the most consecutive jumps or the longest jump.

Adults and teens in the twenty-first century use pogo sticks for fitness and in the extreme sport of Xpogo. With high-tech sticks, Xpogo riders do amazing backflips and jump as high as 10 feet (3 m). They also go for distance. *Guinness World Records* lists the longest marathon on a pogo stick as 206,864 bounces, achieved by James Roumeliotis in Costa Mesa, California, in 2011. He reportedly bounced for twenty hours and thirteen minutes.

Brother, Can You Spare a Dime

—E.Y. (Yip) Harburg and Jay Gorney, 1930, for the musical Americana

CHAPTER THREE
PLAYING THROUGH HARD TIMES: THE 1930S AND THE 1940S

Following the stock market crash of 1929, the nation was plunged into the Great Depression. Millions of Americans lost their jobs and their homes. Banks went broke, and a devastating drought brought crop failure and extreme poverty to Oklahoma and Texas. All over the United States, out-of-work Americans stood in lines at charity soup kitchens to get a bite to eat.

The quickly expanding world of radio and movies provided millions of Americans with entertainment to take their minds off their troubles. Adults and children alike were glued to weekly radio dramas such as *The Lone Ranger*. They flocked to movies such as *Gone with the Wind* (1939) and *Casablanca* (1942).

Facing page: The Lone Ranger was a popular radio show and a successful television show later as well. Advertisers used the character and his horse Silver to sell everything from breakfast cereal to savings stamps, as shown in this 1955 poster (*opposite*).

MiLESTONES

1932 Kansas-born Amelia Earhart becomes the first woman to pilot a solo flight across the Atlantic Ocean.

1933 Franklin Delano Roosevelt is inaugurated as the thirty-second president of the United States. His administration puts New Deal economic policies into effect to put Americans back to work and to turn around the failing US economy.

1933 Prohibition ends with the passage of the Twenty-First Amendment to the Constitution.

1933 Adolf Hitler, leader of the Nazi Party, becomes chancellor in Germany, setting the stage for World War II.

1939 World War II begins in Europe when Nazi Germany invades Poland. Italy and Japan side with Germany.

1939 *Gone with the Wind* premieres. This Civil War-era romance becomes one of the most popular movies of all time.

1941 Japanese warplanes bomb the US naval base at Pearl Harbor, Hawaii, on December 7. The next day, the United States declares war on Japan, thereby entering World War II.

1945 President Roosevelt dies in office, and Vice President Harry Truman is sworn in as president. The war in Europe ends in May. Truman orders the atomic bombing of the Japanese cities of Hiroshima and Nagasaki in August, bringing an end to the war in the Pacific.

Then, in 1941, the United States entered World War II (1939–1945), and thousands of GIs (soldiers) went to fight in Europe and the Pacific. Back home, most resources—gasoline, steel, cloth, and basic foods—went into manufacturing armaments and feeding and clothing the troops. This resulted in shortages of gasoline, clothing, and meat at home. As in the 1930s, Americans found solace in mass entertainment and simple pleasures.

IN FOR A DIME, IN FOR A DOLLAR

Depression-era desperation fueled get-rich-quick schemes. Worn out by trying to make ends meet, Americans grabbed at anything that might bring in a little money. And chain letters promised to bring in a lot. The frenzy started in Colorado in the spring of 1935, with Denver's Prosperity Club, also known as the "Send-a-Dime" chain letter. Nobody knows who sent the first letter, which began, "This chain was started in the hope of bringing prosperity to you." It went on to list six names and addresses. The recipient crossed off the top name and mailed that person a dime. Then the recipient added his or her name to the bottom of the list, made five copies, and mailed them to five more people. (Copy machines had not yet been invented, so each letter had to be written by hand or typed.) If all went according to plan, the recipient could receive 15,625 letters, each containing a dime. Big money!

In no time, the Denver post office system was flooded with as many as ninety-five thousand extra pieces of chain letter mail. Postal employees sorted the mail around the clock. The chain letter mania spread to other cities, and chain letter "factories" sprang up everywhere. For a small fee, secretaries typed letters, some of which requested not just a dime but a dollar. A news correspondent described a rush on a chain letter factory in Springfield, Missouri: "Society women, waitresses, college students, taxi drivers, and hundreds of others jammed downtown streets. Women shoved each other roughly in a bargain-counter rush on the chain headquarters."

Chain letters circulated in the tens of millions. But most people received nothing. Somebody almost always broke the chain, and millions of letters containing dimes lay unclaimed in piles in post offices. The US government

◀ Crowds gather at Loew's Grand theater in Atlanta, Georgia, for the premiere of *Gone with the Wind* on December 15, 1939.

tried unsuccessfully to prosecute a few promoters who had started some of the chain letters, and by 1936, the craze was over.

CRAZY FOR PINBALL

During the Depression, many an out-of-work man and boy spent an afternoon forgetting his troubles in a pinball parlor. Pinball parlors were similar to modern video game arcades. They were noisy places, buzzing with excitement. Lined up in rows, the machines featured flashing colored lights, bells, and gaudy images imprinted on the pinball playfields. Manufacturers gave their machines names such as Baffle Ball, Humpty Dumpty, and Triple Action.

In an era before television, the flash and dazzle provided a cheap thrill. The machine had a colorful playfield under glass, slanted slightly toward the player. The object was to hit and sink small steel balls into holes on the playfield. The player dropped a penny into the machine and pulled a spring-loaded launcher to put the balls in play. (One penny bought five to seven balls.) The player operated

▲ Pinball fever first gripped the nation during the Great Depression. Most Americans saw no harm in the game, though some viewed it as a dangerous form of gambling in disguise. Here, a group of men maneuver to win a game.

flippers to hit the balls. He could also physically bump the machine to direct the ball where he wanted it to go. When all the balls rolled downward and into the drain at the bottom of the machine, the game was over.

People could not get enough pinball. Soon there were machines in soda fountains, penny arcades, and cafés. By the 1940s, many parents were complaining that pinball was bad for kids—that it kept them from more wholesome sports and encouraged foolish spending. Pinball also became a gambler's sport, and the popularity of the game waned. Electronic pinball made a bit of a comeback in the 1990s, but video games soon ruled.

WOULD YOU LIKE TARTAR SAUCE WITH THAT?

Even during hard times, college students had time for some crazy hijinks. For example, in 1939 Harvard University football captain Lothrop Withington Jr. bragged that he had once eaten a live fish. Fellow students offered to pay him ten dollars to repeat his stunt. Students gathered in the dining hall to watch. Withington held up a live, wiggling goldfish. He tilted back his head, dropped it into his mouth, chewed it up, and swallowed it. Ugh! Legend says he sat down to a *cooked* fish dinner right afterward.

The news spread to other colleges. One guy swallowed six fish. A student at the University of Pennsylvania swallowed twenty-five. Gulping down the fish whole, without chewing, made things go faster. A Kutztown (Pennsylvania) State Teachers College student swallowed forty-three fish in fifty-four minutes (and was promptly expelled). A student at Clark University reportedly set a record, swallowing eighty-nine goldfish at one sitting.

Before long, authorities were speaking out. State lawmakers introduced bills to protect goldfish. The US Public Health Service warned that the fish might transmit diseases and parasites such as tapeworm. The novelty wore off quickly, and the fad disappeared the same year it had started.

ON THE EDGE OF THEIR SEATS

During the 1930s and on into the 1940s, every American kid's idea of the perfect Saturday afternoon was to head to a movie matinee to watch the latest episode of a thrilling serial. For a quarter, they could take a seat in the darkened theater, popcorn in hand. First, they would be treated to cartoons featuring Bugs Bunny, Popeye, or other cartoons. Next came a newsreel (a black-and-white eyewitness news film). After that, a B-movie monster film would often follow.

Then came the moment everybody waited for—the newest installment of the current serial. This might be a thrilling gunslinger western, with a cowboy hero

▲ Going to the movies in the 1930s and the 1940s could fill an entire afternoon, with everything from cartoon characters such as Bugs Bunny to newsreels, monster movies, and sing-alongs to entertain the audience—all before the feature film even started!

such as Tom Mix riding down dastardly outlaws. Or it might be dashing actor Buster Crabbe starring as Flash Gordon. Along with girlfriend Dale Arden and companion Dr. Zarkov, Flash traveled into outer space to a sinister planet called Mongo. The audience cheered the heroes and hissed at the villains.

Theaters showed a new fifteen-minute episode every week. Episodes always ended with a cliffhanger. They left Tom Mix cornered by forty bandits or

Flash Gordon's girlfriend tied up and about to be put to death by the evil Ming the Merciless. Moviegoers had to wait in nervous expectation for the following week's episode to find out what happened next.

KILROY WAS HERE

A bald-headed graffiti character with a long nose peering over a wall was everywhere in the 1940s. American soldiers first scrawled the image and the phrase "Kilroy was here" on military ships and docks to show that an American GI had been there.

With incredible speed, Kilroy's image began to appear all over the world. It was found scrawled on everything from the girders of the New York–New Jersey George Washington Bridge to the Arc de Triomphe in Paris, France. It even appeared in the Marshall Islands in the Pacific Ocean. In several American hospitals, doctors about to deliver babies found Kilroy drawings on the mother-to-be's stomach! But with the end of World War II in 1945, Kilroy largely disappeared.

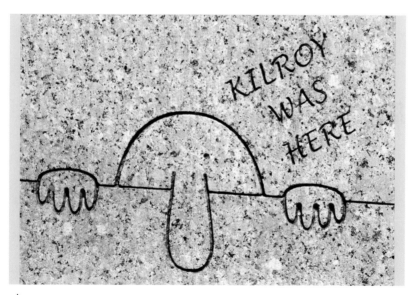

▲ In a nod to the pervasiveness of the Kilroy character during World War II, the character is part of the US National World War II Memorial, established in 2002 in Washington, DC.

Rock and roll music, if you like it, if you feel it, you can't help but move to it. That's what happens to me. I can't help it.

—Elvis Presley, n.d.

CHAPTER FOUR
PHONE BOOTHS AND HULA-HOOPS: THE FABULOUS FIFTIES

With the end of World War II, the United States experienced a rapid growth in wealth and prosperity in the 1950s. The population swelled too, with millions of babies born to returning soldiers and their wives. Known as the baby boomers, this generation of kids grew up in the nation's new suburbs. Moms took care of the family's home life while dads went off to work.

The new prosperity meant that middle-class Americans could afford a nice house, a car, and the newest gadget of all—a television set. TV brought a host of popular shows and advertising into American homes. TV and records also introduced people to a wild new kind of music called rock 'n' roll. Elvis Presley's sexy dance moves and Buddy Holly's wailing rockabilly tunes shocked adults and delighted teens. Fads—from toys and TV shows to rock 'n' roll—were all about those new kids and teens on every block.

Facing page: Unlike other white pop stars of the 1950s, Elvis Presley moved his hips and lower body when he danced and teen girls went wild for him. Many parents and other adults found his movements to be startlingly suggestive.

MiLESTONES

1950 The United States enters the Korean War.

1951 J. D. Salinger's coming-of-age novel, *Catcher in the Rye*, is published. The book is highly controversial for its frank treatment of sex and adolescent rebellion. Teens love it.

1952 Dr. Jonas Salk first tests the polio vaccine, which ultimately eradicates the paralyzing disease in the United States.

1953 General Dwight D. Eisenhower, retired World War II military hero, is sworn in as president of the United States.

1953 Senator Joseph McCarthy becomes chairman of the Senate's Permanent Subcommittee on Investigations. As anti-Communist fever rages in the United States, McCarthy's subcommittee conducts a ruthless pursuit of Communists. False accusations ruin the lives of countless innocent Americans.

1953 The Academy Awards ceremony is broadcast on television for the first time.

1954 In a landmark decision, the US Supreme Court rules in *Brown v. Board of Education* that racial segregation of public schools is unconstitutional.

1955 The release of the record "(We're Gonna) Rock Around the Clock" by Bill Haley and His Comets ushers in the era of rock 'n' roll.

1955 Walt Disney's *The Mickey Mouse Club* debuts on television. That same year, Disneyland opens its gates in Anaheim, California.

1956 Rock 'n' roll idol Elvis Presley takes the world by storm. His first chart-topping record, "Heartbreak Hotel," is followed by dozens more.

1959 Alaska and Hawaii become the forty-ninth and fiftieth states in the Union.

But the era was not all fun and good times. Underneath the sunny surface lay tension and a dark undercurrent of fear. The United States and the Communist Soviet Union had entered the Cold War (1945–1991)—a tense political and military standoff between the world's two superpowers. Anti-Communism reached a fever pitch while racism remained a stain on the fabric of the nation.

CALLING ALL STUDENTS

In the days before cell phones, telephone booths occupied street corners in every city and town. The glass booths were just big enough for one or two people. Fun-seeking students at a junior college in California decided to see how many people could cram into a booth at once. Thirty-two students at Modesto Junior College crammed into one booth. Thirty-three college fraternity brothers in Oklahoma City, Oklahoma, jammed into one booth while a crowd of fifteen hundred spectators cheered them on. Booth stuffing had rules (sort of). Some rules said the phone booth had to have a phone in it. Others said the stuffees had to be able to actually place a call. Sometimes, the kids lay horizontally on top of one another with legs sticking out the door. Sometimes, they just curled up and crammed themselves in any old way.

A NEW SPIN ON FUN

Many observers say the ultimate fad of all time is the Hula-Hoop. The inspiration was a bamboo hoop kids used in gym classes in Australia. Arthur Melin and Richard Knerr—founders of the California company Wham-O Manufacturing Company—figured why not make hoops out of plastic for American kids? These two guys already knew they could create a winner. After all, they had introduced the Frisbee to the world in 1957.

◀ At Memphis State University in Tennessee in 1959, twenty-six Sigma Kappa sorority members crowded into a phone booth.

Hula-Hoops have gone in and out of fashion ever since the 1950s. *Life* magazine devoted its June 16, 1972, edition to the revival of fads from the 1950s—with a Hula-Hoop on the cover.

Fast-forward one year. Melin and Knerr developed the Hula-Hoop, naming it after the Hawaiian hula dance with its swaying hip moves. The polyethylene Hula-Hoop became so popular so quickly that Wham-O was soon producing twenty thousand of them a day. Hula-Hoop contests were not far behind. At a Hula-Hoop Derby in New Jersey, a ten-year-old spun a hoop ten thousand times without stopping. Kids learned to spin hoops around their waists, both arms, and even their necks at the same time. In 1958 ten-year-old Mimi Jordan, national Hula-Hoop champion, drank milk and ate a sandwich while breaking the world record.

In less than two years, Wham-O had sold 100 million Hula-Hoops. And like the Frisbee, the Hula-Hoop just keeps going. In 1967 the company added steel ball bearings inside the hoop, for a *schwoop-schwoop* sound as it spun. The new, improved hoops sold millions. Hula-Hoop fever came back in the 1980s as a nostalgia item. The hoops resurfaced in the twenty-first century, with larger and heavier models. Hula-Hoops these days have become a popular form of exercise and are also incorporated into dance routines and circus acts.

An audience in Los Angeles watches the first-ever full-length color 3-D film, *Bwana Devil*, on opening night at the Paramount Theatre in 1952.

o compete with America's love affair with the television, Hollywood came up with 3-D movies—soon to be known as deepies. In 1952 an excited audience at a movie theater in Los Angeles put on cardboard 3-D glasses to watch *Bwana Devil*, the first-ever stereoscopic film. This movie told the story of two man-eating lions in Africa, and to the moviegoers in their 3-D glasses, the lions seemed to jump off the screen. The audience loved it. Loads of publicity followed, and Americans stood in long lines to see the movie. In its first few months, the film brought in about $5 million.

Other 3-D movies followed, most of them involving scary effects with monsters, weapons, and attacking animals. The 1953 horror film *House of Wax* was the first major studio release in 3-D. It was a much better movie than *Bwana Devil* and was hugely profitable. Starring legendary horror actor Vincent Price, the story involved a wax museum in which the figures turn out to be actual murder victims, covered in wax. The 1954 hit *Creature from the Black Lagoon* featured a scaly monster that reached out at audiences with its webbed, clawed hands.

Eventually, movie audiences began to complain that 3-D gave them headaches. They did not like wearing the cardboard glasses, either. Attendance dropped off, and by 1954, studios were releasing flat-screen versions of movies shot in 3-D just to get people back to the movies.

Technology has come a long way since the cardboard glasses era. The 2009 blockbuster *Avatar* and the 2013 film *Planes* were made in 3-D. And you can even stream 3-D movies on your television, desktop computer, or tablet at home.

CRUISIN' MAIN STREET

In the fifties, teen culture was all about cars. Driving gave kids new freedom and independence. Kids lucky enough to own a car (or to borrow Dad's) piled their friends into hefty steel-and-chrome Chevys and Buicks. From Detroit to LA and in small towns all over the nation, Saturday night was the time to cruise Main Street. Some called it "dragging the Main," or "riding the Avenue." Scores of cars, filled with kids, crawled slowly up and down the street, windows rolled down with rock 'n' roll blaring from car radios. In some neighborhoods, cruising with headlights on meant you already had a date. If your parking lights were on, it meant you were looking.

To take a break, drivers would pull into a drive-in restaurant for a burger and a Coke. The driver gave his order into a speaker, and a carhop (sometimes on roller skates) hooked a tray onto the driver's side of the car and delivered baskets of fries and frosty drinks. Movie director George Lucas later immortalized scenes like this in the 1973 movie *American Graffiti*.

Some "greasers"—rebellious car-obsessed kids with greased-back hairdos—took car culture to a more dangerous level. In T-Birds and other racy cars, they staged illegal street races. But for most teens, cruising Main Street was the route to fun and—with luck—romance during the 1950s and into the 1960s.

KING OF THE WILD FRONTIER

The legendary American hero Davy Crockett was king of television in the 1950s. The real Davy Crockett was a Tennessee frontiersman, soldier, and congressman in the early 1800s. He was killed in the Battle of the Alamo in 1836, during the Texas Revolution (1835–1836).

On television, Davy Crockett first appeared on the *Disneyland* show in 1954. Played by tall, handsome actor Fess Parker, Davy Crockett was a backwoods hero dressed in fringed buckskin and a fur cap with the tail of a raccoon in back. He was a straight talker, a brave fighter, and a champion of the underdog. Walt Disney Productions was quick to capitalize on the show's popularity. In no time, kids could buy Davy Crockett lunch boxes, toothbrushes, bath towels, and coonskin caps. Kids also went wild for fringed buckskin shirts and toy muskets

Actor Fess Parker posed with raccoons and his iconic coonskin cap in this 1955 publicity shot for the short-running but hugely popular *Davy Crockett* television show. Parker played the popular backwoods character in five hour-long episodes, which aired on the ABC television station from December 1954 to December 1955.

like Davy Crockett's. Crockett-themed items earned $100 million in sales in 1955 alone.

The phenomenon lasted about a year. But anybody who kept one of those original coonskin caps probably has a valuable collector's item. In 2004 Parker donated his original cap to the Smithsonian Institution National Museum of Natural History in Washington, DC. And in 2011, an original cap in its original box (which would have sold for less than $10 in 1954) sold at auction for $600!

Don't trust anyone over thirty.

—Jack Weinberg, student political activist, referring to the youth culture of the 1960s, n

CHAPTER FIVE
FLOWER POWER: THE SIXTIES

The 1960s was a time of youth, fun, rebellion, war, tragedy, and profound social change. In 1960 the nation elected its youngest president to date, forty-three-year-old John F. Kennedy—and saw him assassinated just three years later. The inspiring leader of the civil rights movement Dr. Martin Luther King Jr. was also killed, in 1968. Rebellious youth questioned the values of their parents' generation. A wild, carefree counterculture of hippies encouraged youth to—in the words of hippie guru Dr. Timothy Leary—"turn on, tune in, and drop out." And the United States sent troops to the Vietnam War (1957–1975), half a world away in Southeast Asia. This war was to drag on for years, claiming thousands of lives and sparking fiery antiwar protests. Alongside the challenges and tragedies of the decade, a youthful, fun-loving spirit prevailed.

Facing page: Rock star John Lennon and his wife Yoko Ono were figureheads of 1960s hippy counterculture. Here, they are pictured in their honeymoon suite in Amsterdam in 1969. The couple spent a week in bed to protest world violence.

MiLeStOneS

1960   The Barbie doll takes the toy world by storm.

1961   John F. Kennedy is sworn in as the thirty-fifth president of the United States.

1962   Astronaut John Glenn, in the *Friendship 7*, becomes the first American to orbit Earth.

1963   President Kennedy is assassinated. Vice President Lyndon B. Johnson is sworn in as the nation's thirty-sixth president.

1963   Supporters of civil rights legislation stage the March on Washington for Jobs and Freedom demonstration, drawing 250,000 people to the nation's capital.

1963   Betty Friedan's book *The Feminine Mystique* fuels the women's liberation movement.

1964   President Johnson signs the Civil Rights Act of 1964, which prohibits discrimination in schools, workplaces, and public accommodations based on race, ethnicity, religion, national origin, and gender.

1964   Dr. Martin Luther King Jr., leader of the nonviolent civil rights movement receives the Nobel Peace Prize. King is killed by an assassin's bullet four years later.

1965   The first American combat troops arrive in Vietnam.

1966   The *Star Trek* series premieres on NBC.

1969   Richard M. Nixon is sworn in as the thirty-seventh president of the United States.

1969   The nation watches on television as *Apollo 11* lands on the moon. Astronauts Neil Armstrong and Edwin "Buzz" Aldrin become the first people to walk on the lunar surface.

1969   The Woodstock Music and Art Fair in Bethel, New York, draws more than four hundred thosand hippies for four days of free-spirited, good-natured sex, drugs, and rock 'n' roll.

1969   Two million Americans observe the Vietnam Moratorium on October 15 to protest the war in Vietnam with street rallies, meetings, and prayers.

DANCE PARTY!

It is the year 1960. On dance floors all over America, teenagers are gyrating wildly to the year's most popular song—"The Twist." A girl leans backward, twisting, while her partner leans forward, in a move called oversway. Other dancers twist down into a squat and back up again.

What made the twist so popular? For one thing, for the first time in social dancing history, you didn't need a partner. You could dance by yourself or with your friends, and nobody cared. For another thing, it was a rebellious move to shake and wiggle your hips in sexualized fashion. In Tampa, Florida, the city council banned the dance, saying it was indecent. President Dwight D. Eisenhower called it immoral.

An older recording of "The Twist" had originally made the dance popular with African American teenagers back in the late 1950s. In 1960 white America heard a new recording by nineteen-year-old Chubby Checker on the nation's most popular television dance show, *American Bandstand*. Adults and young people alike loved the dance. At a New York dance club called the Peppermint Lounge, society folks did the twist. Rumor had it that even elegant, cultured First Lady Jackie Kennedy was twisting in the White House. By 1962, a succession of new dances—the hully gully, the pony, the locomotion, and the mashed potato—were hot, and the twist faded away.

Rhythm-and-blues megastar Chubby Checker does the twist in ▶ 1965. The R&B singer is known for popularizing the dance move with his 1960 cover of a Hank Ballard song also called "The Twist."

SO UGLY THEY ARE CUTE

If you could go back in time and peek into early 1960s' college dorm rooms, you would see troll dolls on just about every desk and nightstand. These ugly yet lovable figures were all the rage, especially with college girls. Troll dolls were originally modeled on fabled Scandinavian folk creatures. They were mischievous, but it was said that if you captured one, it gave you good fortune.

Danish woodworker Thomas Dam created the first troll doll in 1959 as a birthday present for his daughter. Soon a Danish toy company was making the doll, and before long, troll dolls were being marketed in the United States. They were variously known as Dammit Dolls (a reference to their originator's name), Dam Things, or Wish Niks. Later versions had colored hair, jewels in their belly buttons, and a range of costumes. You could even buy an entire troll village, complete with rocks, caves, and trees. Troll dolls were so popular that high school sports teams used them as mascots. In 1963, when pilot Betty Miller replicated Amelia Earhart's famous transatlantic flight of 1932, she took a troll doll with her. In a short time, the troll doll became the second-biggest-selling doll of the 1960s, behind the more glamorous Barbie doll. But by June 1964, the troll craze had waned.

In the twenty-first century, vintage troll dolls are collectibles. Some people go a little overboard with them. In 2013 the TV show *My Crazy Obsession* featured a woman who had collected more than three thousand of the dolls. She noted, "They're so ugly that they're cute."

BEATLEMANIA

On February 9, 1964, a record-setting 73 million American TV viewers tuned in to *The Ed Sullivan Show*. Teenage girls held their breath as emcee Sullivan announced, "Ladies and gentlemen—the Beatles! Let's bring them on!" Wild screams erupted in the TV studio as the curtain opened to reveal four skinny, mop-headed, British guys with guitars and drums. The Fab Four—John Lennon, Paul McCartney, George Harrison, and Ringo Starr—had officially launched Beatlemania in the United States.

Nowadays, the group's tidy dark mod suits and hairstyle seem so conservative that it is hard to imagine how radical they were at the time. The Beatles heralded a new, free look and attitude. Their mop-top haircuts, mid-length and bowl-shaped, were a radical shift from the short haircuts of the 1950s. Instead of button-down shirts and loose-fitting suits, the Beatles sported the trendy London mod look, with collarless suit jackets and tight-fitting pants. They wore ankle-high, pointy-toed Beatle boots instead of lace-up shoes. As the decade progressed, they moved on to bright flowered shirts, hippie love beads, and longer hair, with mustaches and beards—and American young people followed their example.

John, Paul, George, and Ringo were funny, irreverent, and ready to try anything. When they visited Indian guru Maharishi Mahesh Yogi and got involved in Eastern mysticism, including Transcendental Meditation, millions followed their lead. In the words of authors Jane Stern and Michael Stern, "The Beatles were the embodiment of 1960s iconoclasm [challenge to traditional customs and values] of all kinds."

▲ The British rock band known as the Beatles took the United States by storm in the 1960s. One of the most influential bands of all time, the group made its mark on music, film, art, and fashion. Fans copied the mop-top hairstyle—considered long at the time— as well as the trim suits and heeled ankle boots favored by the band.

TRIPPY HIPPIE LIGHT

The sixties counterculture was all about other-worldly mental and visual effects induced by hallucinogenic drugs popular at the time. Lava lamps captured the mood. The tall, cone-shaped glass lamps were filled with clear or colored liquid. A glob of white or colored wax lay at the bottom. The base held an electric bulb and a metal coil. When the light was switched on, the bulb lit up the liquid. Very gradually, the metal coil heated. When the wax in the liquid got warm, it began to move and slowly take on different shapes. The mesmerizing show went on for as long as the lamp was lit.

Englishman Edward Craven Walker invented the lava lamp in 1964, calling it the Astro lamp. In 1965 Walker sold the US rights to his invention to an American company, which renamed it the Lava Lite. Hippies and counterculture wannabes flocked to buy the trippy lights, which sold by the thousands. Although they have lost fad status, Lava Lites are still alive and well. In fact, the year 2014 marked the fiftieth anniversary of their invention.

SMILE!

What is not to love about a bright yellow smiley face? In the late 1960s, Americans were sporting little metal buttons on their collars and T-shirts with slogans of all kinds. In 1969 button manufacturer N. G. Slater Corporation came out with a new one—a simple, cartoonlike image of a happy face. By 1971 the smiley face was everywhere. Nurses in hospitals, kids on the playground, and politicians on the campaign trail wore the buttons. N. G. Slater sold several million buttons that year alone. Related merchandise followed—smiley faces on coffee cups, stationery, cookie jars, and even trash cans. By the late 1970s, sales of the smiley-face button had dwindled. But the smile icon has never really disappeared. Check out the emoticons on your tablet!

◀ Modern-day lava lamps are still a popular room decoration.

CHAPTER SIX

MOOD RINGS AND DISCO DANCERS: THE 1970s ME DECADE

s the 1970s dawned, the hippie movement was at its height. Americans all over the country were protesting the war in Vietnam, which dragged on until 1975. Many people wanted relief from the tragedies they saw all around them—the unpopular war, the political assassinations of the 1960s, and the Watergate scandal of political corruption that gripped the nation in the early 1970s. Feeling that large-scale social change was doomed, Americans were preoccupied instead with self-fulfillment. They turned to disco dancing, spiritual gurus, and wacky fads of all stripes. In fact, American writer Tom Wolfe coined the term "Me Decade" to describe the era's self-absorption.

"The beat that goes . . . Me . . . Me . . . Me . . . Me."

—Tom Wolfe, "The 'Me' Decade and the Third Great Awakening," New York magazine, August 23, 1976

Right: Tom Wolfe is an influential American author and journalist, who observed that the United States of the 1970s was obsessed with self. Known for his dapper look, he is pictured here at his home in New York City.

MiLeSTONeS

1970 Americans celebrate the first Earth Day.

1970 During antiwar riots at Kent State University in Ohio, the National Guard opens fire and shoots thirteen students, killing four.

1972 Francis Ford Coppola's *The Godfather*—a riveting gangster movie later ranked as one of the best American movies of all time— hits movie theaters.

1974 President Richard M. Nixon resigns in the wake of impeachment proceedings arising from the Watergate scandal. Vice President Gerald Ford is sworn in as the nation's thirty-eighth president.

1975 The Vietnam War ends.

1976 The nation celebrates its bicentennial.

1977 George Lucas's first *Star Wars* movie launches to phenomenal success. Sequels, T-shirts, dolls, and other spinoffs soon follow.

Actor John Travolta *(right)* epitomized the disco craze after starring in the 1977 dance movie *Saturday Night Fever*. In the film, he plays Tony Manero, a young man who leaves behind the boredom and disappointments of daily life when he dazzles on the disco dance floor.

IN THE MOOD

Beware if it turned black. That meant you were tense, irritable, and full of despair. If you were happy and relaxed, it turned blue. If you were nervous, it became yellow. This little emotion detector of the jewelry world was called a mood ring. The ring's hollow glass "stone" contained heat-sensitive liquid crystals that changed color in response to skin temperature. Sometimes, temperature is an indicator of mood, but sometimes, it is not. For laughs, some people heated up their rings in a toaster oven for a happy blue or put them in the refrigerator to turn them black.

The ring was a hit. It tapped into a fascination with all things spiritual and psychological. Marketing wiz Joshua Reynolds came up with the idea for the ring. Introduced in 1975 at New York's fashionable Bonwit Teller, the store sold one thousand of them in one day. In the next few months, Americans bought fifteen million mood rings. The rings ranged from cheap imitations costing a few dollars to 14-karat gold models that sold for $250.00. Even *Peanuts* was in on the game. In one cartoon strip, Peppermint Patty got so mad at Charlie Brown that her mood ring exploded! But the fad was short-lived, and in a few months, it was over.

"HEY BABY, WHAT'S YOUR SIGN?"
—*"What's Your Sign? Is a Retro Pickup Line," 1970s*

CRAZY FOR DISCO

In the 1970s, disco (from the French word *discotheque*) was king. Disco was a lifestyle and a look. Guys wore tight-fitting three-piece polyester suits and sported gold chain necklaces and lots of hair mousse. They danced with girls in slinky wrap dresses, platform shoes, and big hair. To the heavy beat of synthesized music and pulsing strobe lights, dancers mastered the hustle and the bump.

In the hit 1977 movie *Saturday Night Fever*, John Travolta in the role of Tony Manero embodied the style and moves of the king of the disco dance floor. In his white suit—and with his sexy, acrobatic dance steps—he grabbed the imagination of the American public, viewers and critics alike. Disco went global and was even more popular than rock 'n' roll. The sound track for the movie, recorded by the Bee Gees, was one of the best-selling sound tracks of all times, and its songs played in clubs everywhere. Disco eventually died out in the 1980s, but the Library of Congress has preserved the movie, for its social impact, in its National Film Registry.

THE WORLD'S TIDIEST PET

In the meantime, California advertising man Gary Dahl started complaining to his buddies one night about pets. You had to clean up after them, train them, and feed them. It would be great to have a pet that required no care at all, right? Joking around, he came up with the idea of the Pet Rock.

Dahl was clever. In 1975 he wrote a thirty-two-page manual called *The Care and Training of Your Pet Rock*. The manual told readers what to feed the rock, how to teach it tricks, and even how to housebreak it: "Place it on a newspaper. The rock will know what the paper is for and require no further instructions." Dahl packaged the potato-sized rock on a bed of straw in a simple cardboard box with air holes. He sold the first rocks at gift shows. Buyers from large department stores snapped them up. Magazines and television picked up on them, and soon Dahl had a full-blown craze on his hands. He was interviewed on radio and in magazines and newspapers. He even appeared with his pet on late night TV's *The Tonight Show*.

Americans loved their Pet Rocks, which came with their own carrying cases, complete with breathing holes.

eat your way Thin?

No question about it, Americans have been obsessed for decades with staying trim. Most health experts agree that if you need and want to lose weight permanently, you have to do it slowly, building new eating habits you can stick with. Nonetheless, many people want instant results. And so an endless parade of fad diets has enticed the nation. Here are just a few examples of diet crazes, past and present.

Grapefruit diet. This 1930s diet advised consuming "fat-burning" grapefruit or grapefruit juice with *every* meal for periods of up to ten days. The cabbage soup diet, another short-term plan that grew popular in the 1980s, took a similar approach. Experts agree that while these diets do result in weight loss, there is no magic in grapefruit or cabbage. Dieters lose weight quickly because the diet plans call for what some deem a dangerously low number of calories per day. In addition, the diets are not well balanced, and they lack proper nutrition.

Liquid protein diets. A range of powdered products (mix with water and drink) promised Americans they could drink their way to slimness. But many Americans thought this meant to avoid eating solid foods altogether, and they got very sick.

Calories Don't Count diet. Dr. Herman Taller's advice in the 1960s was to stop counting calories and eat foods high in fat and protein. He sold his "magic" capsules to unsuspecting consumers. But they proved to be full of nothing but safflower oil, and the US Food and Drug Administration (FDA), which regulates the safety and labeling of food and medicines, shut down Taller's business.

Atkins diet. Stock up on protein (meat, eggs, and cheese), this 1970s diet advised, and cut back severely on grains and pasta. Similar diets included the Zone, Protein Power, and the Scarsdale diet. Many doctors warn this high-fat approach to eating can put dieters at risk for elevated cholesterol levels, which contribute to heart attacks and stroke.

Cookie diet. A diet based on cookies—what is not to like? In 2006 Dr. Sanford Siegal introduced his program, which prescribed eating six of his special, nutritionally fortified (and not-very-sweet) cookies per day. That, plus a very light daily dinner of "real" food, promised fast and permanent weight loss. Copycat diets soon popped up. Like other fad diets, this one resulted in weight loss mostly because the daily caloric intake was extremely low. Too few calories left many dieters tired, cranky, and hungry.

Most Americans got a good laugh out of the fad—and Dahl became a millionaire. And the rock recently came back on the scene. Once again, you can buy a Pet Rock, complete with leash and instruction booklet.

NOW YOU SEE IT . . .

All you needed was a good pair of sneakers and maybe a mask. Then you stripped completely naked and ran at top speed through a public place or gathering. Streaking got its start on college campuses. Students at Harvard University in Massachusetts streaked through an anatomy class wearing only surgical masks. A group of guys from Columbia University in New York streaked through a girls' dorm at nearby Barnard College. Fifteen of the girls joined them.

The fad soon spread beyond college campuses. A man streaked through the chambers of the Hawaii state legislature, calling himself "streaker of the house." Robert Opel even streaked the 1974 Academy Awards ceremony. The host of the show, suave British actor David Niven, reacted smoothly: "Ladies and gentlemen . . . . Just think, the only laugh that man will probably ever get is for stripping and showing off his shortcomings."

▲ British actor David Niven *(front)* reacted calmly and with humor as streaker Robert Opel flashed the peace sign at the 1974 Academy Awards ceremony in Los Angeles. Opel was a photographer and the owner of an art gallery. He posed as a journalist to get into the event, which was televised to millions of Americans.

Here and there, streakers were arrested for indecent exposure. But often, streaking was viewed as a harmless prank. After a few months and a lot of streaking, the shock value wore off and the fad screeched to a halt.

GOOD BUDDIES

"Breaker, breaker, this is First Mama!" First Mama was First Lady Betty Ford's handle (or nickname) on CB (citizens band) radio. Like her fellow CB lovers, she used trucker's lingo to talk on this two-way communication system. A lot of CB slang was police-oriented. Originally, long-distance truckers used the CB radio frequency to warn one another about speed traps. They referred to highway patrolmen as Smokeys (as in Smokey Bear), and a police officer on a motorcycle as Evel Knievel (in reference to a popular stuntman).

The Federal Trade Commission (FTC) first opened the CB frequency in 1947 to give people without telephones a way to communicate over short distances. Truckers picked up on it in the early 1970s, and by 1976, 650,000 people per month were applying to the FTC for a CB license. Sales of the radio kits skyrocketed, with a peak of an estimated $1 billion by the end of that year. Cell phones have since replaced CB radio in most American cars and homes. But truckers still love it!

The keynote was greed: the underlying philosophy was image over reality.

—Charles Panati, Panati's Parade of Fads, Follies, and Manias, 1991

CHAPTER SEVEN
THE HAVE-IT-ALL YEARS: THE 1980S AND THE 1990S

I n the 1980s and the 1990s, Americans were on a spending spree, ready to "shop till they dropped." They did not worry about credit card debt, and financial scandals were front page news. Alongside the greed and financial corruption of the era, the growth of technology led to a wide range of new electronic games and toys. Computer technology was leaping forward too. The Internet was within reach for most people by the mid-1990s, and by the end of the decade, most Americans were using e-mail instead of the postal service to communicate. Around the globe, more than 45 million people were surfing the Internet.

Young people of the 1980s and the 1990s were the biggest users of the new technologies. They were the biggest spenders too. Companies aimed scores of products at young buyers, who turned many of them into fads.

Facing page: Electronic video games, an outgrowth of the exploding technology scene of the 1980s, replaced the pinball craze of earlier decades. The little yellow Pac-Man character was the star of the biggest game fad of the era.

MiLeSTONeS

1981   Ronald Reagan is inaugurated as the fortieth president of the United States. He serves two terms.

1982   Steven Spielberg's movie *E. T. the Extra-Terrestrial*—the story of a lovable alien stranded on Earth—is a box office sensation.

1983   Sally Ride, aboard the space shuttle *Challenger*, becomes the first American woman in space.

1983   Author Alice Walker receives the Pulitzer Prize for her novel *The Color Purple*.

1989   George H. W. Bush is sworn in as the forty-first president of the United States.

1990   The United States launches the brief Persian Gulf War (Operation Desert Storm) against Iraqi installations in Kuwait.

1993   William Jefferson Clinton is inaugurated as the forty-second president of the United States. He serves two terms.

1994   Jeff Bezos founds Amazon.com, the nation's first online book retailer.

1995   Pierre Omidyar founds the online auction site eBay.

1995   In Oklahoma City, Oklahoma, a bomb rips apart the Alfred P. Murrah Federal Building, killing 168 people. In 1997 Timothy McVeigh is convicted of the crime and put to death in 2001.

1999   Two student assassins kill twelve fellow students and a teacher at Columbine High School in Littleton, Colorado.

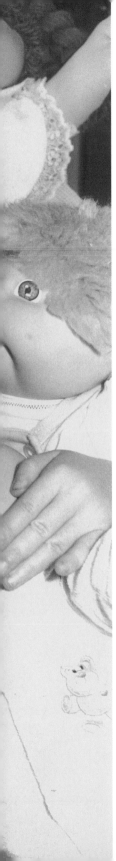

CALL OUT THE RIOT SQUAD

During the Christmas shopping season of 1983, a violent frenzy erupted over a bunch of odd-looking dolls known as the Cabbage Patch Kids. With big, round vinyl heads; stubby noses; fat cheeks; and soft, huggable bodies, these dolls were a must-have for many kids. Xavier Roberts, a twenty-one-year-old art school student, designed the dolls and sold them to the Coleco toy company. Several things made the dolls unique. No two dolls were exactly alike, with variations in clothing, hair, and skin color—even in dimples and freckles. Each doll had its own name. The first one was named Hailey Theeuwen.

The popular fiction behind the dolls was that each one was born in a magical cabbage patch. Customers did not simply buy the dolls, they adopted them. The doll came with a birth certificate and adoption papers. The new owner swore an oath to be a good parent to the doll. Then the owner sent the signed papers back to Coleco, and a year later, the doll received a birthday card.

By 1983 the demand for the Cabbage Patch Kids was so great that the factory could not keep up. That is when the riots started. People would do almost anything to get their hands on a doll. At Zayre's discount store in Wilkes-Barre, Pennsylvania, one thousand shoppers waited in line for eight hours to get the dolls. The manager armed himself with a baseball bat for protection when the angry crowd mobbed the store. One woman suffered a broken leg in the crush. *Time* magazine reported on a near riot in 1983 at Hills Department Store in Charleston, West Virginia. The store manager said, "[Shoppers] knocked over the display table. People were grabbing at each other, pushing and shoving. It got ugly." Predictably, the frenzy died down. By 1986 the dolls were no longer in high demand. But not before Coleco had made sales amounting to more than $6 million!

◄ Cabbage Patch fever spread rapidly across the United States in late 1983. The fad even crossed the ocean to the United Kingdom, where frenzied Christmas holiday shoppers fought to buy the dolls, available at only a handful of stores.

LITTLE, YELLOW GOBBLERS

The 1980s is considered the golden age of the video arcade. As in the pinball arcades of earlier decades, video arcades were usually big, noisy places full of flashing lights and chatter. Guys and girls met to hang out and to play the games. Each game had its own machine, and players stood at the console and fed quarters into the slot.

The biggest game of them all featured a peculiar little hero: a yellow circle with a big, chomping mouth. His name was Pac-Man. Players guided Pac-Man through an electronic maze, chasing down pac-dots, pellets they gobbled up to win points. When all the pac-dots were eaten, Pac-Man moved on to the next stage. Roaming through the maze were Pinky, Blinky, Inky, and Clyde. They were ghosts—enemies of Pac-Man. If they touched him, the player lost a life.

Launched in 1980, Pac-Man was wildly popular with girls and boys. In its first eighteen months, the machines gobbled up an estimated $1 billion in quarters. The game spawned mugs, charms, wallets, sheets, lunch boxes, and other merchandise. An animated television series followed, and "Pac-Man Fever" was a top ten on the *Billboard* Hot 100. Pac-Man also came out as a home video game and as a handheld video game. Billy Mitchell of Hollywood, Florida, reportedly played the first perfect game of Pac-Man. After six hours straight, he reached the 256th screen and earned a score of 3,333,360!

THRILLER MAN

Has there ever been a pop icon quite like Michael Jackson? In the opinion of countless critics and fans, the answer is undeniable: never. One observer called Jackson a "pure entertainment machine." Certainly, many say this one-of-a-kind singer-dancer-songwriter *was* the 1980s.

Images of Jackson in his trademark tight pants and stylish hats, wearing one sequined glove and matching socks, touched off a fashion fad all over the United States. After Jackson appeared in the video for the song "Beat It" (1983) wearing a red leather jacket, everybody had to have one. Jackson's dance moves, including his trademark backward-sliding moonwalk, were copied around the world. Even Michael Jackson dolls appeared on the market and became collectible.

Michael Jackson (*center*), originally a child star of the Jackson Five pop band, was everywhere as a solo performer in the 1980s. Americans loved everything about him, copying his fashion choices and his slick dance moves such as the moonwalk.

Jackson's 1982 album *Thriller* and the related horror-movie-style video were groundbreaking. As late as 2010, *Vanity Fair* magazine reported that "'Thriller' is thriving on YouTube, where one can view, along with the original, scores of 'Thriller' dance tutorials and re-enactments . . . . The dance has become an annual . . . ritual in major cities around the world, with initiates in ghoul makeup aping Michael's moves en masse; the current record for largest dance of the undead is 12,937, held by Mexico City."

EHHHHH! MACARENA

You couldn't go to a dance club, a party, or a wedding without hearing this song. The 1990s Latin-style hit "Macarena" was a song and a dance. The song was first recorded by a Spanish flamenco pop duo—two guys who called themselves Los Del Rio. (The song title refers to a neighborhood in Seville, Spain.) The song, as well as its accompanying music video, became a huge hit in Spain. Soon the song made its way to the United States, where it was an instant hit. The video featured dancers doing the Macarena, a super-simple dance that just about anybody could do. The dance popped up everywhere—on cruise ships and schoolyards as well as at parties. Even the 1996 US women's gymnastics team performed it. The moves were promoted as healthy exercise with the phrase "Swing your way to health with the Macarena!"

By the end of 1996, the song had sold more than four million copies. Finally, the Macarena got played so often, in so many places, that people got sick of hearing it, and its popularity faded. Still, it is like riding a bicycle—once you learn, you do not quite forget how it goes.

VIRTUALLY ALIVE

Remember the Pet Rock of the 1970s? Fast-forward two decades to the Tamagotchi—the world's first virtual pet. In the late 1990s, these egg-shaped pets, with their cute animal faces, migrated from Japan, where they were developed, to the United States. The name Tamagotchi comes from *tamago*, the Japanese word for "egg."

All over the country, kids were suddenly on call 24–7. The pets responded (virtually) to how much attention they got (or did not get). Their owners had to (virtually) feed them regularly, put them to sleep, groom, and train them. If neglected, the pets got sick, displaying sad faces. They could even die a virtual death. The craze eventually died out, but in the twenty-first century, you can get—what else?—Tamagotchi apps for your smartphone.

AN INTELLIGENT TOY

Larger but every bit as adorable as a Tamagotchi pet was the Furby. This electronic creature became the most wanted toy of the 1998 Christmas gift season. Furry, owl-like Furby was part cuddly plush animal, part robot. Not only did it respond to sound and touch, but it also seemed to learn. A new Furby spoke mostly Furbish, its own language. But it was programmed to say more and more words in English, bit by bit, as you played with it. A hit with kids as well as with adult collectors, Furby sold 1.8 million dolls in 1998. It topped its own record the following year with an amazing 14 million sold. Is there a Furby stashed away in your house?

Let US Get Fit!

Americans have long chased a dream of being fit. Most see fitness as a road to health and strength, while others just want to look good. Like losing weight, getting fit requires hard work—in the form of daily exercise. But many people are always looking for an easier path to success. Over the decades, plenty of fitness crazes have sprung up.

1940s Relaxacisor. This device delivered a mild electric shock to whatever body part it touched, causing muscle spasms. Users attached pads—connected by wires to a control panel—onto their hips, stomachs, and buttocks and used control knobs to administer the shocks. It was billed as a "no-effort" way to firm and tighten muscles. People suffered serious health effects from the shocks, and the FDA finally banned the device in 1970.

1950s vibrator belts. These contraptions, which resembled a large automobile fan belt, were guaranteed to jiggle away fat. The user (usually a woman) stood in front of the machine and positioned the belt around her backside. The vibrations supposedly trimmed the hips and thighs.

1970s Richard Simmons's *Dance Your Pants Off!* **video.** This workout actually is good exercise. But because the TV exercise guru gave it such an outlandish spin with his glitzy outfits and over-the-top personality, many people did not take him seriously. Still, Simmons had plenty of fans.

1990s ThighMaster. Actress Suzanne Somers famously demonstrated this machine on TV infomercials. The device was simple—two pieces of metal tubing bent into a loop and connected by a hinge. The user squeezed it between the knees to shape the thighs.

The Millenium Hawaii Chair. This chair, with a seat that rotated at different speeds, purportedly gave the user a hula-style workout. The advertiser claimed, "If you can sit, you can get fit." Exergaming also became a hot trend with the introduction of a range of video fitness games that help players stay active and get fit while having fun. With interactive controllers, exergamers can go solo or play with other people as they engage in virtual activities such as twirling Hula-Hoops or swinging at tennis balls.

More people now have mobile telephones around **the world than have access to a flush toilet.**

—Tim Worstall, "More People Have Mobile Phones Than Toilets," Forbes, March 23, 2013

CHAPTER EIGHT

FLASH MOBS AND WEBKINZ: THE MILLENNIUM

With the coming of the new millennium, social networking took off, with Facebook, Twitter, Tumblr, and YouTube leading the pack. The web was growing by leaps and bounds. By the year 2010, the search engine Google—which launched in 1998—had indexed one trillion unique URLs. About one-fourth of all the people in the world were using the Internet. Meanwhile, the web was going mobile, starting with the 2007 rollout of Apple's iPhone. Smartphones and apps ruled. By 2013 Apple alone had an estimated nine hundred thousand apps and counting. And with the dominance of the Internet, fads were springing up literally overnight, even as a global economic recession brought hard times to families around the globe.

CUDDLY AVATARS

What a genius idea—a pet with a double life, a soft toy that kids could snuggle with *and* a virtual pet they could play with online. When the Ganz toy company introduced Webkinz in 2005, these "pets" became an instant hit. The soft plush toys, sold in stores, came in an array of animal forms, from cute, brown foxes to brightly colored dogs to the blue-winged Blufadoodle. Each pet came tagged with a secret code that gave the owner access to Webkinz World, a site where the pet's virtual counterpart "lived." The pet owner's job was to keep virtual Caramel Lion or Green Seadragon well fed, happy, and healthy. To do that, owners could buy food and other necessities with KinzCash earned by playing games and fulfilling tasks on the site. Tasks might include collecting gems and other items or completing the Game of the Day.

Facing page: Smartphones rule twenty-first-century communication. With a range of apps at their disposal—and with lightning speed—people can share information and plan socially networked events within a matter of hours, if not minutes.

MiLeSTONeS

2001 A new millennium arrives!

2001 George W. Bush is sworn in as the forty-third president of the United States. He serves two terms.

2001 Apple Computer introduces the first iPod.

2001 On September 11, Islamic terrorists hijack four planes and crash two of them into New York City's World Trade Center and another into the Pentagon near Washington, DC. The fourth plane crashes in a field in Pennsylvania. In all, three thousand people are killed.

2003 US forces invade Iraq.

2003 The first social networking site, Myspace, launches.

2004 Facebook launches.

2005 YouTube launches, allowing users to store and share videos online.

2006 Twitter launches.

2007 Apple Computer introduces the first iPhone.

2007 Democrat Nancy Pelosi becomes the first woman speaker of the US House of Representatives.

2009 Barack Hussein Obama is sworn in as the forty-fourth president of the United States. He is the nation's first African American president and is elected to two terms.

2011 US Special Forces locate and kill Osama bin Laden, head of the Islamist militant group al-Qaeda and mastermind of the September 11 attacks.

2013 The US Supreme Court paves the way for federal recognition of same-sex marriage when it overturns the Defense of Marriage Act (DOMA).

Flash mobs started in the United States and quickly spread around the world. Here, a flash mob in Vilnius, Lithuania, gathers to dance in a flash mob competition.

By 2006 Webkinz reportedly had one million online accounts, and sales have continued to soar. These toys are still wildly popular, and even adults get hooked on the online games late at night.

FLASH IN THE PAN

In 2003 *Harper's* magazine senior editor Bill Wasik decided to stage a spontaneous mass event. He contacted a large group of people in New York City, where he worked, and told them to go to four different neighborhood bars. There, they would receive instructions on what to do next. Wasik then told all 130 people to show up at the same time in Macy's rug department. When approached by a salesperson, they were supposed to say they lived together as a group and were shopping for a large rug for their warehouse loft. Needless to say, they caused quite a stir in the rug room, and newspapers quickly reported the phenomenon.

The next mass gathering, also arranged by Wasik, involved two hundred people who converged on the lobby of a Hyatt hotel in New York City and applauded all together for about fifteen seconds. With the Macy's and Hyatt events was born the flash mob.

The idea of a flash mob is for a large group of people to assemble at a predetermined public place, more or less spontaneously. They do something wacky or surprising for a short period of time and then disperse. Flash mobs have delighted unsuspecting passersby all over the world. In markets in Spain, for example, flash mobs suddenly break into operatic song. In major cities all over the world, "Gangnam Style" dancing has broken out to celebrate the K-pop craze that originated with South Korean singer Psy. In Toronto, Canada, a flash mob staged a pillow fight in the middle of the street.

The first flash mobs were organized via cell phone or word of mouth. Since then, super-sized flash mobs are often organized by groups such as Improv Everywhere. This group staged the classic Frozen Grand Central, where a huge group stood frozen in place in New York's Grand Central Station. They also staged the No Pants Day event, when flash mobbers in New York City shocked onlookers by boarding a subway en masse, minus pants. Corporations, movie companies, and political organizations also organize professional flash mobs for publicity or to promote a cause. These are sometimes referred to as smart mobs, and the fad still seems to be going strong.

SOMETHING OLD, SOMETHING NEW

Around 2012 teens began to devise dramatic and public "asks" to prom, launching the promposal fad. Students have done everything from investing in planes flying banners over sports events to packing school hallways with balloons and huge signs.

One guy found a unique way to combine an old fad from the 1990s with the new promposal idea. At lunchtime in his school's crowded cafeteria, Terry approached his intended date dressed as Ash Ketchum, a hugely popular Pokémon character. He recited a Pokémon-inspired poem and opened a Poké Ball that read, "I choose you! Maxine, prom?" Of course, she said yes.

BRACELET FEVER

Do you have a collection of Silly Bandz? These brightly colored, stretchy bracelets were originally designed in Japan as novelty rubber bands, all in animal shapes. When Robert J. Croak, founder of Brainchild Products, saw them, he had an idea. If they could be made larger and a bit thicker, he figured they would make great children's bracelets. In 2008 Croak's Silly Bandz hit the market. By 2010 Croak was selling the bracelets by the millions. His company installed twenty-two phone lines just to keep up with the orders. Croak told *Business Week* magazine, "I have the hottest toy, the hottest fashion product on earth . . . . We don't advertise. All we do is viral marketing. This is happening on its own."

BEING BOARD

In 2007 bored British teenagers Gary Clarkson and Christian Langdon posted a photo of their "lying down" game on Facebook. In the photo, they both lay face down, straight and rigid, with their arms held against their sides. The idea—called planking—caught on all over the world. People began competing with one another to see who could plank in the most unusual or ridiculous places. Soon social media was full of photos of people planking everywhere—across the countertop at a McDonalds, atop a bicycle, on top of walls or pipes, even on

▲ Planking can happen just about anywhere. Here, a group demonstrates the move at Chicago's popular Cloud Gate sculpture (fondly known as the Bean) by British artist Anish Kapoor.

Santa's lap at the mall. One group combined planking with the Tebowing fad. One of the guys planked across the shoulders of three other guys who were imitating football quarterback Tim Tebow's famous pose on one knee, head down, in prayer on the field.

"a HUNDreD Years FroM NOW PeoPLe WiLL WONDer WHY SO ManY PHotoS OF tHeir ancestors inVoLVe tHe SUBJect StanDinG in the BatHrOOM HoLDinG a tHin rectanGULar DeVice at SHOULDer LeVeL."

—*Happygirl22 post on wittyprofiles.com, referring to the 2013-2014 craze for posting "selfie" photos on the Internet, n.d.*

4. Ken Hakuta, *How to Create Your Own Fad and Make a Million Dollars* (New York: William Morrow, 1988), 157.

6. Richard A. Johnson, *American Fads* (New York: Beech Tree Books, 1985), 10.

8. *Merriam-Webster OnLine*, s.v. "twenty-three skiddoo," accessed February 26, 2014, http://www.merriam -webster.com/dictionary/twenty-three%20skiddoo.

11. "Clara Bow," *Wikipedia*, last modified December 29, 2013, http://en.wikipedia.org/wiki/Clara_Bow.

12. Paula Becker, "Dance Marathons of the 1920s and 1930s," *HistoryLink.org*, August 25, 2003, accessed June 26, 2013, http://www.historylink.org/index.cfm?DisplayPage=output.cfm&file_id=5534.

15. *Guinness World Records*, "Most Bounces in a Pogo Stick Marathon (Male)," accessed June 24, 2013, http://www.guinnessworldrecords.com/world-records/1/most-consecutive-pogo-stick-jumps-(male).

19. Paul Sann, *Fads, Follies, and Delusions of the American People: A Pictorial Story of Madnesses, Crazes, and Crowd Phenomena* (New York: Bonanza Books, 1967), 98.

24. "Elvis Presley Quotes," *BrainyQuote*, accessed August 9, 2013, http://www.brainyquote.com/quotes /authors/e/elvis_presley.html.

32. "Don't Trust Anyone over 30, Unless It's Jack Weinberg," *Berkeley* (CA) *Daily Planet*, April 6, 2000, http://www.berkeleydailyplanet.com/issue/2000-04-06/article/759.

33. "*American Experience: Summer of Love*," *PBS.org* clip, televised by PBS on April 23, 2007, http://www .pbs.org/wgbh/amex/love/sfeature/timeline_human.html.

36. Liane Bonin Starr, "Watch: A Woman's Stash of 3,000 Creepy Troll Dolls on *My Crazy Obsession*: The Season Finale Focuses on Toys 'So Ugly They're Cute,'" *Hitfix*, May 8, 2013, http://www.hitfix.com /starr-raving/watch-a-woman-stash-of-3-000-creepy-troll-dolls-on-my-crazy-obsession.

36. "The Beatles," *EdSullivan.com*, accessed December 14, 2013, http://www.edsullivan.com/artists/the -beatles.

37. Jane Stern and Michael Stern, *Jane & Michael Stern's Encyclopedia of Pop Culture: An A to Z Guide of Who's Who and What's What, from Aerobics and Bubble Gum to* Valley of the Dolls *and Moon Unit Zappa* (New York: HarperPerennial, 1992), 43.

39. Tom Wolfe, "The 'Me' Decade and the Third Great Awakening," *New York Magazine*, August 23, 1976, http://nymag.com/news/features/45938.

41. Jaundrea Clay, "'What's Your Sign?' Is a Retro Pickup Line," *Ledger.com*, February 10, 2008, http:// www.theledger.com/article/20080210/NEWS/802100335?p=1&tc=pg.

42. Geoff Williams, "Top 25 'It' Products of All Time: #25—the Pet Rock," *DailyFinance*, February 6, 2009, http://www.dailyfinance.com/2009/02/06/top-25-it-products-of-all-time-25-the-pet-rock.

44. Julian Biddle, *What Was Hot: A Rollercoaster Ride through Six Decades of Pop Culture in America* (New York: Citadel Press, 2001), 124.

46. Charles Panati, *Panati's Parade of Fads, Follies, and Manias: The Origins of Our Most Cherished Obsessions* (New York: HarperPerennial, 1991), 429.

49. Otto Friedrich, "The Strange Cabbage Patch Craze," *Time*, December 12, 1983, http://www.time.com /time/magazine/article/0,9171,921419,00.html.

50. "Michael Jackson Live in Tokyo 1987" Youtube video, 8:18, posted by "Alexandre Decamps," June 29, 2011, http://www.youtube.com/watch?v=iUjxio518CQ&feature=endscreen.

51. Nancy Griffin, "The *Thriller* Diaries," *Vanity Fair*, July 2010, accessed August 11, 2013, http://www .vanityfair.com/hollywood/features/2010/07/michael-jackson-thriller-201007.

54. Tim Worstall, "More People Now Have Mobile Phones Than Toilets," *Forbes.com*, March 23, 2013, http://www.forbes.com/sites/timworstall/2013/03/23/more-people-have-mobile -phones-than-toilets.

58. "Promposal Stories: Teen Recites Pokemon Poem, Asks Date to Prom," *HuffintonPost.com* video, 3:29, posted by Taylor Trudon, April 29, 2013, http://www.huffingtonpost.com/2013/04/29/promposal -stories-teen-re_n_3178852.html.

58. Susan Berfield, "The Man behind the Bandz," *BloombergBusinessweek*, June 10, 2010, http://www .businessweek.com/magazine/content/10_25/b4183064453633.htm.

59. Happygirl22, "Selfies Quotes," wittyprofiles.com, accessed February 6, 2014, http://www.wittyprofiles .com/quotes/selfies/5.

SELECTED BIBLIOGRAPHY

Batchelor, Bob. *The 2000s: American Popular Culture through History.* Westport, CT: Greenwood Press, 2009.

Batchelor, Bob, and Scott Stoddart. *The 1980s: American Popular Culture through History.* Westport, CT: Greenwood Press, 2007.

Becker, Paula. "Dance Marathons of the 1920s and 1930s." *HistoryLink.org,* August 25, 2003. http://www.historylink.org/index.cfm?DisplayPage=output.cfm&file_id=5534.

Best, Joel. *Flavor of the Month: Why Smart People Fall for Fads.* Berkeley: University of California Press, 2006.

Biddle, Julian. *What Was Hot: A Rollercoaster Ride through Six Decades of Pop Culture in America.* New York: Citadel Press, 2001.

Drowne, Kathleen Morgan, and Patrick Huber. *The 1920s: American Popular Culture through History.* Westport, CT: Greenwood Press, 2004.

Hakuta, Ken. *How to Create Your Own Fad and Make a Million Dollars.* New York: William Morrow, 1988.

Johnson, Richard A. *American Fads.* New York: Beech Tree, 1985.

Lovegren, Sylvia. *Fashionable Food: Seven Decades of Food Fads.* New York: Macmillan, 1995.

Lupiano, Vincent DePaul, and Ken W. Sayers. *It Was a Very Good Year: A Cultural History of the United States from 1776 to the Present.* Holbrook, MA: Bob Adams, 1994.

Oxoby, Marc. *The 1990s: American Popular Culture through History.* Westport, CT: Greenwood Press, 2003.

Panati, Charles. *Panati's Parade of Fads, Follies, and Manias: The Origins of Our Most Cherished Obsessions.* New York: HarperPerennial, 1991.

Reilly, Edward J. *The 1960s: American Popular Culture through History.* Westport, CT: Greenwood Press, 2003.

Sagert, Kelly Boyer. *The 1970s: American Popular Culture through History.* Westport, CT: Greenwood Press, 2007.

Sann, Paul. *Fads, Follies, and Delusions of the American People: A Pictorial Story of Madnesses, Crazes, and Crowd Phenomena.* New York: Bonanza Books, 1967.

Sickels, Robert. *The 1940s: American Popular Culture through History.* Westport, CT: Greenwood Press, 2004.

Smith, Martin J., and Patrick J. Kiger. *Poplorica: A Popular History of the Fads, Mavericks, Inventions, and Lore That Shaped Modern America.* New York: HarperResource, 2004.

Stern, Jane, and Michael Stern. *The Encyclopedia of Bad Taste: A Celebration of American Pop Culture at Its Most Joyfully Outrageous.* New York: HarperCollins Publishers, 1990.

——. *Jane & Michael Stern's Encyclopedia of Pop Culture: An A to Z Guide of Who's Who and What's What, from Aerobics and Bubble Gum to* Valley of the Dolls *and Moon Unit Zappa.* New York: HarperPerennial, 1992.

Young, William H., and Nancy K. Young. *The 1950s: American Popular Culture through History.* Westport, CT: Greenwood Press, 2004.

——. *The 1930s: American Popular Culture through History.* Westport, CT: Greenwood Press, 2002.

FOR FURTHER INFORMATION

BOOKS

Cooper, Gael Fashingbauer, and Brian Bellmont. *Whatever Happened to Pudding Pops? The Lost Toys, Tastes, and Trends of the 70s and 80s.* New York: Perigee, 2011.
Read about toys, clothes, activities, food, entertainment, and just plain silly stuff from the 1970s and the 1980s.

The Decades of Twentieth-Century America series. Minneapolis: Twenty-First Century Books, 2010.
This series of ten titles for young adult readers examines the cultural climate of the twentieth-century in the United States, exploring trends and popular culture while also discussing each decade's politics, technological advances, economy, and more.

Robinson, Matthew, and Jensen Karp. *Just Can't Get Enough: Toys, Games, and Other Stuff from the 80s That Rocked.* New York: Abrams Image, 2007.
This lighthearted book provides lots of fun facts about a wide range of toys from the 1980s, complete with lots of color photos.

Spangenburg, Ray, and Kit Moser. *Teen Fads: Fun, Foolish, or Fatal?* Berkeley Heights, NJ: Enslow, 2003.
This book offers a serious look at fads past and present and how they can influence teen lives.

Szpirglas, Jeff. *They Did What?! Your Guide to the Weird and Wacky Things People Do.* Toronto: Maple Tree Press, 2005.
Cartoonlike illustrations accompany short descriptions of a wide variety of oddball fads, stunts, incidents, and characters.

Westerfeld, Scott. *So Yesterday.* New York: Razorbill, 2004.
This thought-provoking novel is an action-filled story about teen trendsetters.

WEBSITES

CrazyFads.com
http://www.crazyfads.com
Read about fads from the past, decade by decade.

MichaelJackson.com
http://www.michaeljackson.com
This is the website for all things Michael Jackson.

Mortal Journey
http://www.mortaljourney.com/trends
Read all about fads and trends from every decade, from 1930s comics to 2010s promposals.

Time.com
http://www.time.com/time/specials/packages/0,28757,2049243,00.html
Take a look at *Time* magazine's picks for the one hundred all-time greatest toys.

VIDEOS

"Chubby Checker—the Twist (Live 1961)." Youtube video. 2:46. Posted by pigcityrecords, February 8, 2012. http://www.youtube.com/watch?v=hbSYDZbFpOM
Watch Chubby Checker do the Twist in the 1960s on Dick Clark's *American Bandstand* TV show.

"Fess Parker—Ballad of Davy Crockett (1955)." YouTube video. 2:15. Posted by warholsoup100, April 20, 2011. http://www.youtube.com/watch?v=txcRQedoEyY
Listen to the 1950s *Davy Crockett* TV show theme song.

"1920s the Charleston." YouTube video. 2:56. Posted by Aaron1912, February 27, 2007. http://www.youtube.com/watch?v=ZJC21zzkwoE
Take a look at how to dance the 1920s Charleston.

"Superman (1948) Columbia Movie Serial Episode One (Part 1 of 3)." Youtube video. 6:44. Posted by hermankatnip, March 5, 2010. http://www.youtube.com/watch?v=YtcUvrJCGao
See the first episode of the classic Superman story. Continue watching the site to see parts 2 and 3.

"Top 10 Flash Mobs." Youtube video. 39:00. Posted by YouTube Trends, April 21, 2011. http://youtube-trends.blogspot.com/2011/04/10-most-viewed-flash-mobs-of-all-time.html
Watch an amazing array of flash mobs deemed the best by YouTube.

INDEX

ABOUT THE AUTHOR

Cynthia Overbeck Bix grew up in Baltimore, Maryland. Family visits to historical sites sparked her early interest in American history, crafts, and everyday life. Now living in California's San Francisco Bay area, she loves to write about anything and everything. In her more than thirty nonfiction books for children and adults, she has covered topics such as fine art, natural science, domestic arts, and American fashion. She has also written how-to books about all kinds of activities, from making impressions of animal footprints to planting a garden. Among her books are *Petticoats and Frock Coats: Revolution and Victorian-Age Fashions from the 1770s to the 1860s* and *Spending Spree: The History of American Shopping*.